Miloli's Orchids

Story by Alisandra Jezek
Illustrations by Yoshi Miyake

RSVP
RAINTREE
STECK-VAUGHN
PUBLISHERS
The Steck-Vaughn Company

Austin, Texas

To Mom, Dad, my two grams,
and to my friends,
especially Jen. —A.J.

To all the children of the world. —Y.M.

Trade Edition published 1993 © Steck-Vaughn Company

Copyright © 1991 Steck-Vaughn Company

Copyright © 1991 Raintree Publishers Limited Partnership

3 4 5 6 7 8 9   95 94 93

Library of Congress Number: 90-42769

Library of Congress Cataloging-in-Publication Data

Jezek, Alisandra.
  Miloli's Orchids/story by Alisandra Jezek; illustrations by
Yoshi Miyake.

  Summary: A young girl faces the life-or-death challenge of saving
her homeland from destruction.
  [1. Orchids—Fiction. 2. Patriotism—Fiction.] I. Miyake, Yoshi,
ill. II. Title.
PZ7.J572Mi   1990   [Fic]—dc20   90-42769
ISBN 0-8172-2784-9 hardcover library binding   CIP
ISBN 0-8114-5209-3 softcover binding   AC

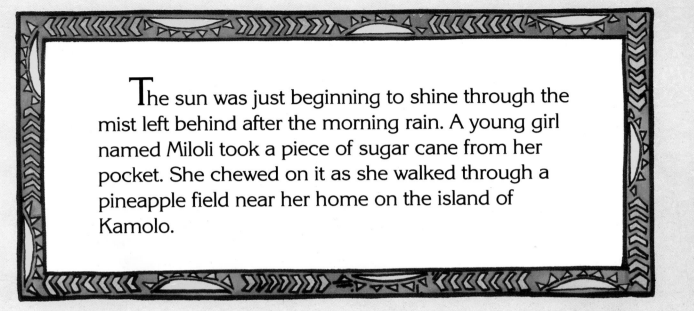

The sun was just beginning to shine through the mist left behind after the morning rain. A young girl named Miloli took a piece of sugar cane from her pocket. She chewed on it as she walked through a pineapple field near her home on the island of Kamolo.

Miloli watched as workers planted pineapple shoots in the damp, warm ground. In the distance, she saw Kihala, the great volcano. Her grandfather, Salep, had told Miloli that the volcano was asleep. Miloli wondered whether Kihala slept with one eye open, waiting.

The day was getting hot, and Miloli decided to look for shade. She walked until she reached the dense coconut grove on the far side of the volcano. After resting for a while, Miloli walked on. Just as she began to realize how far she had wandered, Miloli became astounded at the sight before her.

There, at her feet, was a field of the most beautiful wild orchids she had ever seen. Their colors danced in the sunlight, overwhelming Miloli. She reached down and picked one delicate blossom for her hair before running off toward home.

Grandfather! Grandfather!" she called.

"What is it, child?" asked Salep.

"Grandfather! A vision! I have found a huge field of orchids at the foot of Kihala! Come quickly!" Miloli begged, out of breath.

"Ah, sit down, Miloli, sit down. I have seen this field of orchids. Let me tell you their story," Salep said.

Salep pointed toward the horizon, to a distant spot on the ocean. "A long, long time ago, people from Kamolo visited that island to the south. The people there were very friendly to our people.

"To seal the bond of friendship, they gave us some of their precious orchid plants. They told us that the plants contained the living spirit of the god Makapa. Makapa would protect us from destruction. But if the orchids were ever destroyed, Kamolo would also be destroyed. Since that time, the plants have grown and multiplied, and Makapa has watched over us."

13

Miloli thought about her grandfather's tale all day. Later that afternoon, she decided to return to the orchid field to be sure it was not just a dream.

As Miloli walked, she felt a rumbling beneath her feet. At first, it seemed like the sound of thunder before a storm, but the sky was clear. Just then, there was a flash of red across the sky. It was Kihala. The sleeping volcano was awakening. By the time Miloli reached the orchid field, fire and ash were flying out of the top of the volcano.

Miloli knew that her family must be worried about her, but all she could think about was saving the orchids—the spirit of Makapa.

How could she save them? She couldn't stop the volcano from erupting. She would have to gather up her courage and as many orchids as she could carry. Then she would have to try to outrun the flowing hot river of lava. Miloli knelt and collected as many orchid plants as her small arms would hold.

By the time Miloli stood up again, the lava had reached the edge of the orchid field. She ran as fast as she could, but it was difficult. Her arms were full, and the ash was choking her and burning her eyes. Surely, she and the orchids would be lost.

Miloli finally reached the coconut trees. Still clutching the plants, she struggled to climb a tree so tall it seemed to touch the sky. Miloli could barely breathe by the time she reached the top. Then she turned to see if the volcano was still spitting fire. Just as suddenly as the eruption had started, it stopped. Kihala was quiet again.

Soon Miloli's family and others on the island reached the coconut tree to rescue her. They helped Miloli to the ground. The child was too exhausted to speak. Everyone was grateful that she was safe, especially Salep, who carried her home.

The next morning, Miloli could hear the rain falling softly. She was happy to be home and safe, but suddenly she remembered the orchids. The field must have been destroyed by the lava, and the plants that she had tried to carry home were left at the top of the coconut tree. The island of Kamolo was doomed!

Just then, Miloli's grandfather appeared in the doorway. He tried to calm her. He said he had something to show her. They returned to the coconut tree that Miloli had climbed.

Salep lifted the child high up into the air. Miloli started to cry. There, where she had left them, were the orchids. They were as beautiful and delicate as before. Their roots had twined and twisted around the branches of the coconut tree. Miloli had rescued the spirit of Makapa. Kamolo would not be destroyed.

From that time on, the orchids grew and multiplied in the treetops—forever safe from Kihala's fire.

Alisandra Jezek wrote **Miloli's Orchids** while she was in the sixth grade. Her inspiration for the story grew out of a science project that she worked on, about how a volcano erupts. Alisandra constructed a model of a volcano and read about some famous eruptions. Her research led her to read more about orchids and the tropical paradise of Hawaii. The words used in the story are similar to Hawaiian names or are words related to orchids. For example, the name *Salep* is a word for dried orchid roots used in medicines.

Alisandra is an only child. She has a chocolate Labrador retriever named Bosco Barney. In addition to her studies at St. Raymond de Penafort School in Mount Prospect, Illinois, Alisandra also studies piano and French. She is an avid collector of rock music, buttons, books, and stickers. She is also a wizard at computer games. Alisandra isn't certain about what she wants to be when she grows up, but she has a keen interest in astronomy, the sciences, and writing.

Alisandra's parents are Noelle and George Jezek.

The twenty honorable-mention winners in the **1990 Raintree Publish-A-Book Contest** were: Della Armstrong of Moyie Springs, Idaho; Alane Benson of McKeesport, Pennsylvania; Jonathan Caton of Flossmoor, Illinois; Gabriel Chrisman of Bainbridge Island, Washington; Christy Druml of Waukesha, Wisconsin; Rebecca L. Emmel of Sandpoint, Idaho; Nicole Estvanik of Enfield, Connecticut; Amanda M. Frank of Slinger, Wisconsin; Lara Garraghty of Goode, Virginia; Andrea Jauregui of Syosset, New York; Aynsley Kenner of Mesa, Arizona; Dharma C. Lawrence of Spring, Texas; Jackie Lyn Leavitt of Idaho Falls, Idaho; Darren Ruthenbeck of Carmichael, California; Tim Schlosser of Durand, Wisconsin; Blake Smisson of Fort Valley, Georgia; Tori Smith of Walkerton, Indiana; Pia Suparak of San Dimas, California; Christy Williams of Mt. Dora, Florida; and Stephanie York of Edmonton, Kentucky.

Artist Yoshi Miyake was born in Tokyo into a family of artists. In 1966, she came to the United States to study design and illustration. The major body of her work consists of children's books. Yoshi loves to travel in the western states, and she collects American Indian art. She lives in Chicago with her Doberman pinscher, Bucky.